UNDERSTANDING FOUNDATIONAL LITERACY AND NUMERACY (FLN)

DR DHEERAJ MEHROTRA

Made with ♥ on the Notion Press Platform
www.notionpress.com

Contents

Preface

Understanding Foundational Literacy and Numeracy (FLN) is a work to depict the clarity of the concept as per the National Education Policy (NEP). The idea is to reflect on the defined spectrum. Broadly conceptualised as a child's ability to read introductory texts and solve fundamental maths problems (such as addition and subtraction). Foundational Literacy and Numeracy are central themes of the NEP 2020.

I am sure the book shall serve the educators to explore the connection in its best heritage and understanding.

Cheers & Happy Learning.

Dr Dheeraj Mehrotra

Author

1

Understanding Foundational Literacy and Numeracy

Literacy at a basic level is also necessary since it enables people to express themselves. Students will struggle to connect with various courses throughout the curriculum if they lack fundamental reading abilities.

If a person has trouble reading and writing, it may significantly impact their capacity to succeed in other areas of their education and life.

Because a child's reading, writing, speaking, counting, arithmetic, and mathematical thinking skills need to be strengthened for them to have a better chance at being successful in life and their careers, learning experiences that are based on play and activities need to put more of an emphasis on these areas. Reading, writing, speaking, counting, arithmetic, and mathematical thinking skills are interconnected.

Which of the FLN's many objectives is considered its highest priority for the immediate future?

Ensuring that every child can read and respond with comprehension, independently write with understanding, develop number sense, mathematical thinking, problem-solving, and reasoning skills, and build number sense and mathematical thinking is the fundamental purpose of the national mission of FLN. FLN's goal is to ensure that every child can read and respond with comprehension.

The end objective of the FLN is to ensure that every kid can read and understand what they read. When faced with a scenario such as this one, one of your key concerns should be the kid's general progress in terms of physical and mental maturation. Improving Students' Learning Outcomes Through Flexible Learning Networks, National Education Policy Act, 2020.

The National Education Policy 2020 acknowledges the significance of early education by stating, "Our top aim must be to achieve universal foundational literacy and numeracy (FLN) in primary school and beyond by the year 2025." The Ministry of Education, Government of India has launched a Foundational Literacy and Numeracy (FLN) Mission and provided guidelines to build literacy and numeracy skills among children at the foundational stage. The programme will be implemented in the mission mode. Administrators and teachers have some queries regarding FLN mission, its implementation and role of various stakeholders in its implementation etc.

Fundamental Literacy and Numeracy Not Just A Skill But A Life Skill! Reading and arithmetic skills are fundamental ones. Thus, a good foundation in these

areas is essential. Not Just A Skill But A Life Skill! Taken separately, reading and writing are the two fundamental pillars of literacy. Literacy may be dissected into its component parts.

In contrast, it comprises a wide array of talents and abilities, including a capacity for arithmetic and comprehension, reasoning, and expression. It is essential to reason logically, discover solutions to issues, and apply the four fundamental operations of mathematics in a pertinent manner to the situation. Having a rational and logical frame of mind is necessary.

This is in recognition that early education is the foundation for later learning. This is a recognition of the significance of getting one's educational career off to a good start at a young age. If this most fundamental learning is not initially accomplished (reading, writing, and arithmetic at the foundational level), the rest of the policy will be utterly meaningless for such a significant proportion of our pupils since it will not be able to help them.

Developing oral language involves expanding conversational skills and improving listening comprehension, oral vocabulary, and oral vocabulary. Oral language development also includes expanding oral vocabulary. Reading and writing can only be honed after acquiring the experience necessary to read and write via interaction with spoken language.

Understanding the relationship between various symbols and the phonemes that those symbols stand for is a necessary step in decoding, which is interpreting written words.

The textuality of the Reading Experience is again an important initiative. This term refers to a child's ability to read a text with accuracy, fluency (automaticity), expressiveness (prosody), and comprehension, which allows the child to extract meaning from the text. Many young people can recognize aksharas, but to read them, they have to do it one at a time.

Reading comprehension may be attained by constructing one's meaning in response to a text and then participating in an in-depth critical examination of that meaning. Reading, understanding, and gleaning information from written texts, as well as interpreting such works, are all included in this domain of expertise.

Writing, the ability to write akharas and words, as well as the ability to register for the sake of expression, are both talents that come within the ambit of this topic.

Ideas that come before numerical values tend to Acquire the ability to count and grow used to the numerical system. The study of numbers and the operations that may be done on them make up mathematics. Gain a grasp of the norms necessary for mastering mathematical processes, such as using a base ten system to represent numbers. This understanding is essential to master mathematical methods.

Measurement is another format which tends to Acquire the knowledge and skills necessary to perform basic mathematical operations such as addition, subtraction, multiplication, and division on integers with up to three digits, such as addition, subtraction, multiplication, and division, and then put those skills to use.

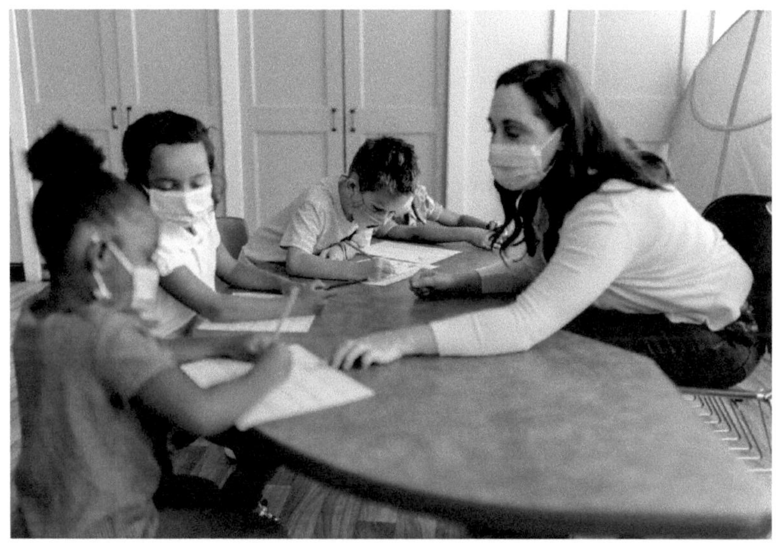

Data Handling under the FLN can recognize and extend fundamental patterns, starting with recurrent forms and continuing to numerical patterns, and the ability to interpret simple facts and information in the context of her regular life activities.

Comprehending the Forms and How They Relate to the Space Around Them Perform fundamental mathematical operations up to three-digit numbers in her or his way and apply these operations to the activities they participate in throughout the day in various situations.

Understanding FLN Better:

As educators, we don't only pick up new information via our own experiences; we also pick up further information as we define different ideas. The order of precedence will be shown in this section in case anything else has been specified.

Language and literacy are the cornerstones around which everything else is constructed. They are the foundations upon which everything else is built. Reading is a skill that must be acquired via a multi-stage process that calls for using a wide range of distinct elements; are you familiar with any of these? Having experience with a foreign language is helpful when it comes to the process of gaining literacy abilities in a foreign language. This is because the process of building literacy abilities in a foreign language may be a complicated procedure.

The following is a list of the most critical factors that have a role in the maturation of core language and literacy skills:

Participating in talks like this is crucial because of the potential for experiences in spoken language to aid in the development of reading and writing ability considerably.

A Consciousness Derived From Phonology: This field of study covers the talents of word awareness, a grasp of rhyming, and an awareness of sounds inherent within words; all of these abilities should naturally evolve via the student's meaningful engagement with language. Another talent that would be considered to fit under this category is the ability to rhyme.

Along with an awareness of print, an understanding of akshara, and the ability to distinguish words, the ability to decode is one of the sets of talents that come within the ambit of this discipline.

In addition to oral vocabulary, reading/writing vocabulary, and morphological analysis of words, this section of the exam for the vocabulary segment incorporates morphological analysis of words. Additionally, the morphological analysis of words is going to be covered in this section of the test.

The capability of comprehending the reading content: This domain of competence comprises not only the understanding of written material, but also the extraction of information from written material and the interpretation of written material. In addition, the competencies required for adequate reading comprehension are included within the area of responsibility for this domain.

The ability to read a text accurately, quickly (automaticity), expressively (prosody), and with comprehension, all at the same time, is referred to as reading fluency. Young people can get a more profound grasp of the material they are reading due to this. When we talk about this talent, we're referring to the capacity to read a text in a manner that conveys expression (prosody).

Getting a Solid Grounding in the Fundamentals of Printing: For young children to develop the capability of comprehension, they need to be presented with a wide range of chances to interact with content that contains a significant amount of print. Writing is a competence that comes under this domain, and it requires not only the talent to write words and aksharas, but also the capability to write to express oneself in written form. This domain also includes the ability to express oneself in spoken form.

A passion for reading and the desire to further one's education are two attributes that are very valuable to possess. Reading successfully requires an interest in various books and other materials and a desire to interact actively with those books and resources.

A working knowledge of, as well as the capability to carry out, the fundamental procedures of mathematics and computing. The ability to reason and apply basic numerical principles to solving problems encountered

in day-to-day living is what we mean when we talk of foundational numeracy. When we talk about "foundational numeracy," this is precisely what we mean. The following is a rundown of some of the most significant aspects and components that may be discovered in early mathematics:

It is essential to know how to count and get used to the system of numbers to comprehend better the concepts that existed before the invention of numbers.

Mathematics is a branch of academic study that focuses on numbers and the many operations that may be carried out on them: Acquire a grasp of the standards that are important for the mastery of mathematical processes, such as the utilization of a system with a base ten to represent numbers. This understanding is necessary to become proficient in mathematical procedures. Having this grasp to complete mastery of the mathematical functions is essential.

Structures, in Addition to Several Other Locations, can do primary mathematics in her or their own manner up to three-digit numbers and apply these principles to the activities they engage in throughout the day in a range of contexts. Perform basic mathematical operations in their own manner up to three-digit integers, including addition and subtraction. Perform essential mathematical functions in their own way up to three-digit integers, including reserve and subtraction.

Learn and use conventional processes for performing mathematical operations on integers with up to three digits, including addition, subtracting, multiplying, and dividing. These operations include adding, subtracting, multiplying, and dividing. Understanding how to do arithmetic operations such as adding, subtracting, multiplying, and splitting integers with up to three digits is essential.

In addition, the Measurement:\sFacts Handling makes it a go as well. This helps to Recognize and build upon fundamental patterns, starting with those that involve repeating shapes and continuing to those that include numbers; grasp basic facts and information relevant to the activities that he or she engages in on a day-to-day basis. The Foundational Reading and Numeracy (FLN) Mission, which was started by the Ministry of School of the Government of India, involved providing guidelines for the development of reading and numeracy skills in children at the foundational level of education.

The project was given the name "Foundational Reading and Numeracy," which is an abbreviation for "Foundational Reading and Numeracy." Mission mode will be used so that the program may be carried out

successfully while it is being carried out. The purpose of FLN, the manner in which it will be implemented, and the roles that different stakeholders will play in its implementation, amongst other topics, have been the focus of a great deal of inquiry on the part of administrators and educators.

2

FLN Activities - At a glance!

The learning objectives for foundational learning have been broken down into three distinct developmental goals:

Goal 1: Health and well-being;

Goal 2: Effective Communicators;

Goal 3: Increasing Leadership Capabilities (Involved Learners).

The FLN has been specified in four domains: spoken language, reading, writing, and numerical literacy. Each class has discussed these objectives, beginning with Balvatika and continuing through Class III.

Reading and mathematics have been mandated as the key areas of concentration by NEP 2020, with the goals of bridging the achievement gap and initiating the process of creating meaningful and pleasurable learning outcomes for students in classes suitable to their ages.

To achieve this objective, on the national level, a mission known as NIPUN Bharath was initiated, with the objective of ensuring that by the year 2025, all children in the country who are enrolled in grades 3 and above have achieved fundamental reading and numeracy skills. This goal was set with the intention of ensuring that by the year 2025, all children in the country who are enrolled in grades 3 and above have achieved these skills. The term "Bharath," which translates to "India," is where the name of the mission derives from in Sanskrit. In order to achieve this goal, a program known as Foundational Literacy and Numeracy is being developed. As a component of that curriculum, the following topics of knowledge and conversation will be covered:

The primary aim of the national mission of FLN is to enable all children to read and respond with comprehension, independently write with understanding, and develop number sense, mathematical thinking, problem-solving and reasoning. The focus is on the holistic development of the child.

At this point, working on developing the core abilities necessary for further learning is required. The educational programs that children participate in should be devised to instil the powers that are essential for the children's physical, cognitive, linguistic, emotional, and social development. The National

Education Policy 2020 has voiced grave worry over the fact that there are around five crore pupils in our nation who cannot read, write, or carry out the four fundamental arithmetic operations.

The long-term educational objectives for pupils who are currently enrolled in primary school have been broken down into the following three main categories:

The first objective is to enhance one's physical health and general well-being; the second objective is to enhance one's capacity for effective communication, and the third objective is to improve one's potential for effective leadership (Involved Learners).

Reading, writing, oral language comprehension, and numerical literacy are the four subcomponents that come together to form the functional level of literacy (FLN). The FLN's newly established organizational structure is comprised of these four factions. The discussion on how to accomplish these objectives over the whole of the course work started with Balvatika and continued to Class III.

An Explanation of the Different Roles and Objectives Carried Out by the FLN goes with a reason to explore Learning that is considered fundamental for a kid is critical because it provides the framework for any further learning that the child will engage in later in life. If, by the time a child reaches the end of Class III, they have not mastered the essential skills of reading with understanding, writing, and doing simple arithmetic operations, then that child will not be prepared for the more challenging courses come after Class III.

Within the constraints of the mission, priority will be given to the following five areas of responsibility: This goes to the resemblance of the NEP Initiatives. In addition to ensuring that children have access to basic education and that they continue their education throughout the foundational years, other important components include building the capacity of teachers, creating student and teacher resources and learning materials that are of high quality and diverse, monitoring the progress that each child is making toward achieving learning outcomes and addressing the nutritional, health, and mental health needs of children. All these components are interconnected and play an essential role in ensuring that children have access to primary education and continue their education throughout the foundational years.

3

FLN Major Objectives

Every kid who takes part in one of FLN's programs will be held to the expectation that they can read, write, and do mathematical calculations at a level that is comparable with the grade level at which they are working. The following is a list of the most important goals that have been formed as a result of the suggestions made in NEP 2020:

To create an environment in the classroom that is welcoming to all students by giving play, discovery, and activity-based pedagogies high priority, connecting the curriculum to the day-to-day living conditions that children experience and integrating children's native languages into lessons taught in a more academic setting.
To empower children to develop into readers and writers who are self-directed, independent, engaged, and motivated; whose reading and writing abilities can be maintained over time; who have comprehension skills in addition to their reading and writing abilities; and who have reading and writing skills that

can be held over time.

To instil in children a grasp of reasoning in the areas of number, measurement, and form; to help children to become self-sufficient in the area of problem-solving through the development of abilities in numeracy and spatial thinking. Those are the goals of this lesson.

To ensure that educational learning material of a high standard and one that is sensitive to the cultural backgrounds of the children is readily available in the children's native, home, or mother language, and to make the most of its potential for teaching and learning purposes; to ensure that educational learning material of a high standard and one that is sensitive to the cultural backgrounds of the children; to ensure that educational learning material of a high standard and one that is (s).

It is of the highest significance to emphasise the ongoing professional development of educators, including but not limited to classroom teachers, principals, and other academic resource people and administrators.

To have meaningful conversations with all relevant stakeholders, including teachers, parents, students, community members, and decision-makers, to provide a solid foundation for learning that can be built upon and developed throughout an individual's life. Portfolios, group and collaborative work, project work, quizzes, role plays, games, oral presentations, and other activities are used to facilitate learning and ensure proper monitoring of each student's current learning level. Other activities include: This is done to ensure that evaluations are carried out "as, of, and for."

To emphasize and place a significant emphasis on elementary school learning, the program will be implemented in mission mode, with the existing mainstream structures being used and improved throughout the process.

At the national level, the implementing agency will be the department of School Education and Literacy, that is housed under the Ministry of Education (MoE), and a Mission Director will serve as the head of the department in this capacity. Both of these divisions are overseen by the Ministry of Education here in this country. The Foundational Reading and Numeracy (FLN) Mission, which was initiated by the Ministry of School of the Government of India, entailed the provision of guidelines for the development of reading and numeracy skills in children at the foundational level of education. These guidelines were intended to encourage reading and numeracy development in young students.

The term "Foundational Reading and Numeracy," which is an acronym for "Foundational Reading and Numeracy," was given to the project when it was first conceived. We will be operating in mission mode in order to ensure that the program is carried out without any hitches while it is being carried out.

The purpose of FLN, the manner in which it will be implemented, and the roles that various stakeholders will play in its implementation, amongst other topics, have been the focus of a significant amount of inquiry on the part of administrators and educators. Literacy is essential to monetary growth in addition to an individual's and a community's overall sense of well-being. Literacy skills that are effective allow individuals to access further educational and job options, which in turn enables them to lift themselves out of poverty and chronic underemployment.

It is vital for people to continually extend their knowledge and gain new skills in order to stay up with the speed of change in our more complicated and fast changing technological environment. The emancipatory capacity of literacy has the ability to translate into greater political engagement, which in turn may contribute to the overall quality of public policy and democracy. In order to meet the challenge of equipping every child with the fundamental literacy and numeracy skills they need to be successful in life, the government of India has launched a national mission for literacy and numeracy that goes by the name National Initiative for Proficiency in Reading with Understanding and Numeracy, or NIPUN BHARAT. This mission is part of India's larger effort to achieve universal proficiency in reading and mathematics. The mission's vision is to create an environment that is conducive to the universal acquisition of foundational literacy and numeracy as a means of ensuring that by the end of Class III, every child will have attained the desired learning competencies in reading, writing, and numeracy. In order to accomplish this, the mission's vision is to create an environment that is conducive to the universal acquisition of foundational literacy and numeracy. This will be achieved by producing a setting that is favorable to the establishment of an environment that enables this setting to be established.

4

Vision of Foundational Literacy and Numeracy Mission

Every child will be given the opportunity to acquire the necessary learning skills in reading, writing, and arithmetic by the time Class III is over, and at the absolute latest, by the time Class V is over. This requirement is to be reached as early as possible. The youngster will have the chance to participate in this activity as soon as is humanly practicable. They will have the opportunity to make use of this opportunity up to the end of the Class V curriculum. Throughout the whole educational experience that they will be taking part in, they will have this opportunity at their disposal at all times. At the earliest practicable date, which is the school year 2026–2027, the mission's objective is to attain Full Literacy and Numeracy (FLN), which stands for "Full Literacy and Numeracy," for all first- and second-grade pupils. The primary purpose of this mission is to establish circumstances that, in as many different ways as possible, will make it easier to accomplish the goal that has been set. To get started on the path that will lead to the realization of this objective, the very first thing that will have to be done is to make sure that favourable conditions will have been formed by the years 2026 and 2027.

In order to ensure that the goals of NEP 2020 are met, the primary emphasis of elementary education will transition to one that places primary emphasis on the holistic development of children through the discovery and development of their ability for creative expression. This change will be made in order to guarantee that the goals of NEP 2020 are achieved. This shall be carried out in the right way so that it is in accordance with the aims of the NEP 2020. It is desired that the education that is made accessible will be all-encompassing, all-encompassing, comprehensive, integrated, comprehensive, entertaining, engaging, and comprehensive. Moreover, all of these characteristics will be present in the comprehensive education. Every child will have access to a learning environment in school that is fair and inclusive, that takes into account the various cultural backgrounds of the students, that satisfies the students' requirements for multiple languages, that takes into account the students' varying academic abilities, and that encourages the students to be active participants in the learning process.

If students are able to demonstrate success in reading, writing, and arithmetic while still in the primary years of school, this will provide them with a solid foundation for continuing their education throughout their whole life. Reading, writing, and arithmetic are the three building blocks of education. Reading, writing, and arithmetic are the three fundamental pillars upon which an education is founded. Reading, writing, and arithmetic are the three essential foundations upon which an education is constructed. Reading is the most important of these three. Throughout the whole of the process of primary education, there is a continued emphasis placed on the overall growth and development of the student. This focus is on the development of the kid as a whole. In order for the lesson to be effective, each and every kid in the classroom has to be content, have confidence in themselves, be thinking, and be open to learning new things.

In addition to the FLN's organizational structure, its administrative and management structures will be discussed below.
The FLN Mission will be carried out by the MOE, and a five-tiered implementation structure will be built at the National, State, District, Block, and School levels throughout all of the states and UTs in the nation. This structure will be used to execute the FLN Mission. The FLN Mission will be carried out with the assistance of this facility. The whole nation will be covered by this system's coverage in its totality. The program will be executed in "mission mode" so that attention can be focused on it, and priorities may be created in order to make certain that it is completed in advance of other activities. The bulk of the program's execution, which will take place over the course of the coming few months, will make use of traditional organizational

structures. This will be the case for the great majority of the program's execution.

The Necessary Steps That Ought to Be Taken Prior to Attempting to Complete the FLN Mission Before Making an Attempt to Complete the Mission of the FLN In the most recent years, one of the most important factors that has contributed to widespread anxiety on a national scale is the fact that children's academic performance continues to be consistently low throughout all stages of their school lives. This has been one of the most significant factors contributing to widespread anxiety. One of the most serious issues that has been creating worry on a national basis in recent years has been this issue.

When pupils have gone too far behind in their schoolwork, it is impossible for them to catch up after they have reached this point since they have already gotten too far behind. The National Education Policy Act of 2020 (NEP, 2020) provides further support for the notion that it is necessary to discover a solution to this enigma. The conundrum refers to the situation in which there is an environmental problem.

In order to attain the aim of guaranteeing that everyone has the core reading and mathematics abilities, it is vital to make sure that everyone has access to education. It has been agreed to continue ahead with the implementation of Vidya Pravesh, which is a school preparation module for pupils in Class 1 that is centered on play and lasts for a total of three months.

The decision to move forward with the implementation was made. This subcomponent will, in a very short amount of time, be elevated to the status of a program that operates throughout the whole of the system. In order to meet the challenge of providing every child with the fundamental literacy and numeracy skills they need to be successful in life, the government of India has launched a national mission for literacy and numeracy that goes by the name National Initiative for Proficiency in Reading with Understanding and Numeracy, or NIPUN BHARAT. This mission is a national mission for literacy and numeracy that aims to provide every child with the fundamental literacy and numeracy skills they need to be successful in life.

The National Initiative for Proficiency in Reading with Understanding and Numeracy (NIPRNU) is responsible for implementing this objective. This goal is a part of India's larger program, which aims to guarantee that all of its residents have a fundamental mastery of reading and mathematics. The mission's vision is to create an environment that is conducive to the universal acquisition of foundational literacy and numeracy as a means of ensuring that by the end of Class III, every child will have attained the desired learning competencies in reading, writing, and numeracy. This will be accomplished by creating an environment that is conducive to the universal acquisition of an environment that is conducive to the universal acquisition of foundational literacy and numeracy. This will be done by providing an atmosphere that is favorable to the universal learning of a fundamental level of reading and numeracy.

This environment will be conducive to the universal acquisition of a foundational level of literacy and numeracy. To achieve this goal, we shall cultivate an environment that is conducive to the literacy and numeracy training of as many people as possible on the most basic level. This setting will be favourable to the learning of a fundamental level of reading and numeracy by all individuals. The objective of this mission is to establish an atmosphere that is favorable to the education of everyone in the world in the foundations of reading and mathematics as a manner of achieving this goal. This will be done as a method of reaching this target. This will be accomplished by constructing a setting that is conducive to the growth of an environment that enables this setting to be created, and this will be done in a way that enables this setting to be generated. This setting will be one that is favorable to the development of an environment that enables this setting to be created. Because of the environment that exists here, the development of this scenario will be made feasible.

The fulfillment of the educational needs of children between the ages of three and nine is the major focus of this mission, and the fundamental aim of this mission is to satisfy that basic need. As a consequence of this, learning gaps will be found along with their potential causes, and a variety of strategies will be utilized, taking into consideration the particulars of the local environment in addition to the variation that exists across the country. This will be done in order to address the learning gaps that have been identified. As a direct consequence of this, learning gaps, as well as the possible factors contributing to such gaps, will become apparent. In addition to this, the goal is to establish a solid link and a smooth transition between the early grade levels of education and the preschool stage throughout the course of the child's educational career. Because of this, the students will have more tools at their disposal to ensure that the time they devote to studying is productively used.

What kind of preparation is required in order to take part in the activities that are being planned by the FLN?

Before a child can start the process of learning to read and write, they need to have reached a specified set of developmental milestones first. These milestones vary from child to child. They are falling farther and further behind in basic reading and writing skills because they have not received the necessary preparation in reading and writing. As a consequence of this, people are put in precarious situations in which they have a competitive disadvantage vis-à-vis everyone else. In addition to this, it is of the utmost importance to introduce the basic concepts of numeracy and arithmetic to children at a young age.

This should take place as early as possible. Learning that is considered fundamental for a kid is important because it establishes the foundations for all later learning that the child will perform. If a child does not master the essential talents required for learning beyond the third grade, such as reading with comprehension, writing, and doing simple arithmetic operations, then that child will not be equipped for the progressively challenging topics of the curriculum. The National Education Policy 2020 recognizes the importance of early education by declaring, "Our main target must be to attain universal basic reading and numeracy in primary schools by 2026-2027." This is an acknowledgment of the value of early education.

This objective is scheduled to be accomplished by the conclusion of the 2026-27 academic year. Literate societies are informed about their communities and actively participate in them. People who have reached a sufficient degree of literacy are able to comprehend and understand information pertaining to their health, which plays a role in the general improvement of such people's states of health.

A community that has a high literacy rate is a dynamic community; it is a community that actively discusses problems, communicates ideas, and as a consequence is more creative and productive. The sharing of ideas, perspectives, and concerns leads to increasing levels of mutual understanding and concern, which ultimately leads to a powerful feeling of community spirit in the long run.

About The Author

Dheeraj Mehrotra, MS, MPhil, PhD (Education Management) honoris causa., a white and a yellow belt in SIX SIGMA, a Certified NLP Business Diploma holder, is an Educational Innovator, Author, with expertise in Six Sigma In Education, Academic Audits, Neuro-Linguistic Programming (NLP), Total Quality Management In Education, an Experiential Educator, a CBSE Resource towards School Assessment (SQAA), CCE, JIT, Five S, and KAIZEN. He has authored over 100 books on topics which include Computer Science, AI, Digital Body Language, NLP, Quality Circles, School Management, Classroom Effectiveness and Safety and security in schools. A former Principal at De Indian Public School, New Delhi, (INDIA), NPS International School, Guwahati, and Education Officer at GEMS, Gurgaon, with an ample teaching experience of over Two Decades, he is a certified Trainer for Quality Circles/ TQM in Education and QCI Standards for School Accreditation/ School Audits and Management. He has also been honoured with the President of India's National Teacher Award in the year 2006 and the Best Science Teacher State Award (By the Ministry of Science and Technology, State of UP), Innovation in Education for his inception of Six Sigma In Education by Education Watch, New Delhi and Education World- Best Teacher Award, BOLT Learner Teacher Award by Air India, 'Innovation in Education Award 2016' by Higher Education Forum (HEF), Gujarat Chapter, among others. He has developed over 150 FREE EDUCATIONAL MOBILE Apps for the Google Play

Store exclusively for Teachers, Students, and Parents. This work has been recognised by the LIMCA BOOK OF RECORDS & INDIA BOOK OF RECORDS as the only Indian to draw that feast. Dr Mehrotra works as a PRINCIPAL at KUNWARS GLOBAL SCHOOL, Lucknow, in India. He has conducted over 1000 workshops globally on "Excellence In Education" integrated with Total Quality Management and Six Sigma, Technology Integration in Education (TIE), Developing towards being ROCKSTAR TEACHERS, including Cyberspace, Cyber Security, Classroom Management, School Leadership & Management, and Innovative teaching within classrooms via Mind Maps, NLP and Experiential Learning in Academics. He is an active TEDx speaker and can be viewed on the youtube TEDx channel.

As a premium UDEMY Instructor, he has developed over 450 courses and caters to over 8 Lakh students from 180 countries.

He can be visited at www.authordheerajmehrotra.com.

Schools may play a significant role in advancing the goals of peace, and there is a strong case for extending the understanding and practice of peace education in traditional schools. After all, conventional education institutions do much more than impart facts and techniques; they also mould individuals' moral and ethical convictions and perspectives on life. Promoting peace education in a conventional school setting calls for a complex strategy.

ABOUT THE AUTHOR

Books By The Same Author

https://www.amazon.in/Books-Dheeraj-Mehrotra/

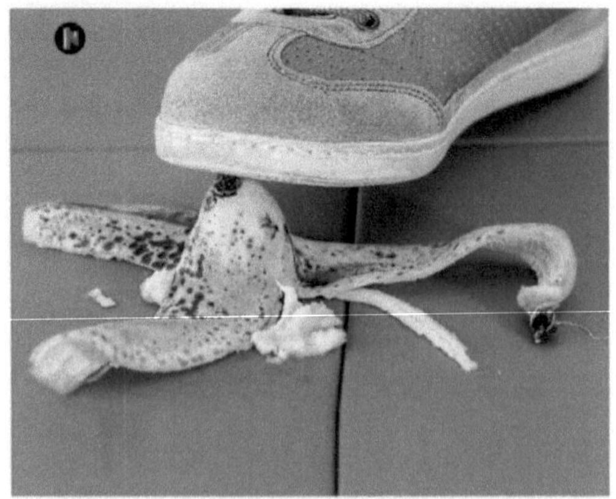

SECURING SAFETY & QUALITY CARING

99 SAFETY AND SECURITY

ANCHORS WITHIN SCHOOLS

DR. DHEERAJ MEHROTRA

A PRIORITY

FOR SCHOOLS

www.authordheerajmehrotra.com

BOOKS BY THE SAME AUTHOR

BOOKS BY THE SAME AUTHOR

A Must For All Home Libraries
Preparing Parenting Mindset For Futuristic Learning
Dr Dheeraj Mehrotra
Paperback: ₹ 99
Available at
flipkart.com
amazon
www.authordheerajmehrotra.com

9 798888 692264

Printed by Libri Plureos GmbH in Hamburg,
Germany